Caught in the Middle

Caught in the Middle

A True Story

Bob & Cindy Titolo

To order additional copies of this book, contact:
Xlibris Corporation
1-888-795-4274
www.Xlibris.com
Orders@Xlibris.com
104519

Acknowledgements

I want to thank my husband, Bob, for putting up with my daughter, Nicole and all his input in helping me write this book. Thank you honey!!!! Also, would like to thank you to my dear friend Myra Hayman who always was there to listen to me when I needed to vent.

I wrote this book in an effort for those that read this they will too find out that a pathological liar can be helped with medications and inpatient treatment. This has been a terrible situation to have to go through years and years of. Learn the signs I looked it up on the internet.

To my grandchildren that I pray for everyday that they have been placed in a descent home with love and care when they were abandoned by their mother and took away from their father.

Introduction

This book is about a pathological liar. A person that will tell more lies than truths. They will lie up to the last minute, and when the truth finally comes out and they are caught in a lie they have no remorse.

Their first response to a question would be to lie for an answer, whether it is necessary or not.

You will see how a liar can get whatever they want by lying. You will also see how people can go years and years without having to work for a living and the effect it has on others.

Chapter 1

Our names are Cindy and Bob Titolo. and one day we were sitting and watching the Casey Anthony trial. The words pathological liar kept coming up and my daughter, Nicole, (Bob's step-daughter) as I told everyone was a habitual liar with a narcissist personality. So I looked on the internet to see what pathological lying was. It fit Nicole to a T.

So now I am going to tell you about another pathological liar that I have, Nicole. Well as a kid she always lied, but I didn't think too much of it as kids do tend to tell tales sometimes. But as she got older they were getting to be more frequent and there was a "NO" in her vocabulary. She did what she wanted to do manipulating and lying to get it.

Then it was 2 days before she was going to be 18 and Bob told me to go look in her room as she was packing all of her things. I went in there when she told me she was moving out with this guy she hadn't known for long, Lee Batts. In fact, a week prior he brought her home and she had overdosed, I had to call the paramedics, as she was supposed to be taking a bath and it was so long I went to check on her and she was blacked out. So the paramedics had to get her out of the tub and take her to the hospital where they pumped her stomach. But yet she told me it was not him that overdosed her and she was going to move in with him. He really didn't have a place to live as he lived with his grandparents who raised him, at least his grandfather as he had remarried so it was his step-grandmother. But she came into the picture much later after his wife had died. But the grandparents raised Lee since birth.

He too was a liar, a user, drug addict, woman beater and the list goes on. Lee's grandfather was a wealthy man and always got Lee out of any trouble he got himself into. In fact, that is why they moved to Florida from Alabama as he was caught on an HBO special about the KKK and his picture was in the special. So they moved down here to protect him.

After a few months of living with his grandfather who was growing tired of them just hanging around and not working, paid for them to have their own apartment. That was short lived. For one they never paid the rent and when Mr. Batts (grandfather) went over to the apartment he found a newspaper stand they had stolen off the street to get the change out. All they were doing with their money was drugs. So after that stunt Mr. Batts moved them, Nicole included back to a different part of Alabama to live.

After she got up there they went to live with his real mother, Sheila, as he got Nicole pregnant and Mr. Batts had his fill. Nicole kept calling us which seemed like every other day for us to send her money via Western Union. She said that they have to buy food, etc. It got to the point that I told her she needed to come back as she was costing us more money living there than it did when she was here and we couldn't afford it. Well I quit sending money and later learned that they were using it for drugs, not that they needed or paid to help with food or board.

This was my first grandbaby as my son was born with cystic fibrosis (incurable lung disease) and he couldn't have children. So we kept in touch with Nicole. But it was always because her and Lee were fighting. Lee actually left her at his mother's house and stayed with another girl for a while.

When my granddaughter was about to be born I went to Alabama to be with Nicole while she had the baby. They had told me to hurry and come as she was having contractions so I took off immediately. I flew up and rented a car from the airport. I drove to Sheila's house and surprised Nicole as she didn't know I would be there that soon. While there, Sheila was the one telling me that the money we sent was used for drugs as she found needles in their room. I guess Lee moved out with the girl as Nicole wasn't doing drugs while she was pregnant and all they did was fight. Nicole got a job at one point at Big Lots but then couldn't work anymore due to her pregnancy. So she stayed with Sheila and her husband. She helped clean and do laundry as Sheila had injured her back on the job and was waiting for a law suit to end.

Well the contractions were false so it was about a week before she had my granddaughter, Brianna. I spent a few more days there so I could have time with the baby as I had to get back to work.

So when they were up there I actually flew them down here twice so I could see Brianna and of course she couldn't come without Lee. So therefore I had to pay for his ticket too. We thought he had a license so when here we let them drive our new car later to find out he didn't have a license. But again liars, they both were.

My son, Jason, with the cystic fibrosis had his own home. He did have some nice friends that looked out for him some also. Scott was one of those friends and Ashley who later Nicole befriended was his girlfriend. I tried to let him live life to the fullest as we never knew how long he would be with us. He was sick all his life but was getting worse and really wanted to just live in his house and be independent as he used to always come and stay with us or his grandmother. So he told Nicole she could move in with him, which I thought was a good idea as he needed the help and she could give it to him and I would be near the baby too. So she, Lee and the baby moved in.

Before they arrived here we had went and fixed up the room and bought a crib and other accessories for Brianna. At first things seemed to be going good. But my son had frequent stays in the hospital so that left Lee, Nicole and Brianna at home by themselves for weeks at a time as that is how long it would take them to get him where he could come home. Every time Jason went in the hospital Lee always beat on Nicole. She took a whole lot of abuse from him. Lee had a lot of tattoos which all had some kind of meaning. He had one on his leg that Nicole always asked what that one was about but would never tell her. One day when he was beating her and so enraged, he said you really want to know what that tattoo is for? He told her that he and this other guy, I think near Birmingham making a drug deal with this black guy. They met in a barn somewhere and they ended up killing the guy, so they both got the tattoo to remind him of I guess his dirty deed. To this day if he said the truth there is an unsolved murder there to which he has never been punished for. One day driving down the road Lee was trying to actually push Nicole out of the car while moving with Brianna watching. But when my son got out he would never touch her. Their neighbors were really good friends to my son and Nicole. The neighbor caught Lee hitting her and said the next time he caught him there was going to be trouble. Lee was always getting into fights especially in the bars when out at night.

The next thing I found out that Sheila sent her other son, Jeremy Lee's brother who also had 2 kids at that time who also didn't work and was useless. Now how could someone do that to a dying person? I guess he was living with her and she had enough of Jeremy so she thought she would send him here to see if maybe he would be different. The house was a small 2 bed room home and Jeremy slept on the couch. Actually Jason liked Jeremy a lot more than Lee as he never really cared for Lee due to his macho attitude. But it was Nicole's boyfriend as he was married years before and never got a divorce, so Nicole never married and Jason put up with him.

Lee would find jobs but would not keep them long, sometimes taking Jeremy with him. I thought they were paying my son to stay there and I found out they didn't give him a dime. They were always having friends come over mostly Jason's friends. Lee started playing pool as he thought he was the next Minnesota Fats. He was fairly good but not all that. So he started going to the bars at night so he could play pool and left Nicole and Brianna at home. They had one car which he always took and Nicole would sometimes have to get her friend, Ashley, to drive her around looking for him, even in the early mornings. Also, Nicole waited on Lee hand and foot, so much it was sickening as he made her. But every time Nicole had any kind of problem she would just call me at work and she wiped her hands clean of it as I would fix it somehow.

I was trying to keep my distance of her as she knew exactly what she could ask and get away with. Well Brianna was supposed to start kindergarten and Nicole made no effort in getting her started or anything. Ashley kept on Nicole as she knew she needed to be in school. So Ashley found the school that she would go to and since it had already started Ashley paid for a tutor to catch her up for a few weeks. If it was not for Ashley I don't know if Brianna would have made kindergarten that year or not.

As my son had his visits in the hospital Lee took full advantage of beating Nicole. Then he started cheating on her. I told her to leave him over 100 times that he was not going to change and she could not change him.

Jason was put on oxygen all the time now and Nicole did take good care of him as he could not do much of anything as he had no air as his lungs were filling up.

Then one day Lee and Jeremy for some reason got into a fight. Lee was beating Jeremy so badly he went running to the neighbors for help. He beat him pretty bad and after that Jeremy went back to Alabama.

Chapter 2

In February of 2001, I get a call to my work and it was my son's neighbor telling me to get to his house that I was needed. I just knew what had happened and I was screaming and crying all the way out the door till I got to the house and the neighbors and Nicole were standing there crying. I had lost my son. Nicole had just gone out in the back yard to let Brianna play on the swing set and when she came back in he was on the floor. She called 911 and they told her how to start CPR on him. He was already dead but she tried that till the paramedics came and declared him dead.

I was just in shock, I knew it was going to happen but it still breaks your heart. Especially as he was a wonderful son, giving, caring and loving. Since I was divorced a few times he took over like he was the man of the house and would protect us. That is how he treated Nicole. I had remarried and had been married for some years and Jason loved my husband, Bob. One time when he was at Tampa General Hospital we received a call around 4:30 a.m. and was told to get down there as he was about to die. So we rushed down and called everyone. He actually called some of his friends to tell them good-bye, it was heart breaking. He then said he could go as he knew that Bob would take good care of me and he didn't have to worry anymore. He really got along well with Bob. He stated this feels really funny as he did not know what dying felt like and to us he didn't seem like he was going to die then but I didn't know. So finally one of the doctors came in and we told him that he was saying his good-byes and the doctor was irate as he told me that they just got Jason in there and who told us that. They hadn't even started any treatment yet. Well nevertheless he lived another 1 ½ to 2 years.

Unfortunately the time had come and we had to make preparations for his cremation and having a service for him. It was stressful as we did not have any money but somehow we made it and I think it was very nice. Nicole gave me a song that he had picked out for me to play at his service which I never knew. It was the song, "Simple Man" by Lynard Skynard and when I heard it I couldn't quit crying. I forget when you know you are dying you can plan some things you want. Nicole picked "Free Bird" also by Lynard Skynard.

Before his death we used to always go out to Picnic Island, a small beach, kind of isolated and would take food and spent many days there. He enjoyed feeding the birds and that is where I put his remains. I also want to be there one day with him. It is such a quiet serene setting, really nice.

That Easter we had a party/service and I put his remains in the ocean where I want to be placed when I die. That was our special place and always will be.

So after dealing with all of that, actually the day Jason passed Nicole said Jason wanted her to have his house which he wanted everyone to have it because when people who really helped him like myself, my mother and Nicole he would always say that. Well it was my house as she never paid him a dime even to live there. But I wanted them to have a house so I wouldn't have to worry and I thought it would give them a good start. WRONG!!!!

Chapter 3

I had to pay $1,500 to put the house in her name as of course they never had any money. Since Jason was no longer in the picture the fighting went on. A month or two after Jason's death, Nicole became pregnant again. She was upset and I was also. They couldn't support themselves let alone another baby. Well she ended up having a baby boy named Lee Lee.

As Jason couldn't have babies, Brianna was his pride and joy. He must of known he was going to die soon as he never liked getting his pictures taken but he took a couple with Brianna. I wish he could have been here for Lee Lee to be born as Nicole would have let him in the room to see his birth which would have been another experience he on his own could never have.

The grandparents frequently came down to visit bringing lots of presents for them, surely money was given too. Mr. Batts made up for Lee's shortcomings. They lived there for probably a year or so and condemned the house, literally. Lee had his friends over all the time or he was gone out to the bars and left Nicole with the kids at home. They had broken a mirror on the side of the house which no one ever picked up, roaches you could not believe, and bathroom wall rotting due to not fixing the plumbing I didn't know about.

Nicole finally told Lee he had to go it was over. I told her to sell the house as they could not even pay the $170 a month mortgage which was quite a few months late and we could not pay for it either. We had to call one of those places that will buy your house no matter what condition it was in and since Jason had put a great amount down on the house and had owned it for so long she received close to $50,000. All of a sudden Lee was behaving and promised her he wasn't going to play pool anymore, etc. He wanted the money. So she tried it again.

Out of that money I made Nicole give me $15,000 as I felt it was due to me as I was supposed to be getting Social Security for him all his life but instead they denied him a few times and I worked two jobs to support us. So when he turned 18 there had been a court case that won due to the child having cystic fibrosis and finally they accepted the fact that it was a terminal disease. So they back paid him to the first time I applied and that is how he got his house.

When she sold the house they all came to live with us until they could find another home to buy. I was looking at some really nice mobile homes in nice parks, so that way she could pay for it and only have lot rent to pay. Plus it was much closer to us as I always seemed to have to run over to their house for some reason like taking her to the store for food or doctor visits for the kids, which got really old after working all day. We found a couple of nice homes they looked at but Lee did not like any of them. I think he had a thing about living in a mobile home. Bob said that lee didn't want to spend the money for that, as he wanted to party with it.

Right off the bat we did not get along. Lee had already started playing pool again and since it was on the other side of town it was hard for him to get rides as they did not have a car then. We would find him on our back porch locked out in the mornings when we woke. He turned around and apologized to Bob and Bob said you are telling the wrong person, you need to tell Nicole that not me.

One night he had to stay outside all night till morning and he had forgotten his pool stick on the porch before going in to bed. At that time we had a Miniature Pinscher that we could never house break and I have to say this made my morning that day. We let him out to do his business but on the way back in he stopped and peed on his pool stick a couple of times as we left the door opened in the house off the porch. He never said a word about it stinking or anything and maybe to this day he doesn't even know but I really thought he got just a little of what he deserved. He thought of himself as being such a great person. His MO was living with different people and not paying anything to live there. He would hop from place to place, as when the person would get tired of him he would move on to someone else to use.

They had not been at our house long as we could tell were not interested in either living on that side of town or it being a mobile home, not really sure. The straw that broke the camel's back was when one morning we all were up and Bob was at work as he was the assistant manager who worked 60 to 70 hours per week. It was around 10:00 and Lee said to me, hey let's get Kathy (their old neighbors) to watch the kids so we can go get some drinks. I was furious as I am thinking here Bob is working all those hours and has bad heart problems as he had a double bi-pass in 1995. Also that day Nicole took the kids to the pet store and bought them a hamster, which we ourselves had too many animals. It was like they were there to stay and blow the money. I called Bob and when he got home he told them they needed to get out because I could not take them anymore.

They were not interested in buying or looking anywhere to live and I had to make the effort every day to go out and look with Nicole. It was just too much as I didn't have very good feelings towards Lee any more. I wanted him out.

When they got out the rumors were flying that they had to sell the house because they were helping us as we were about to lose ours. Another lie!!!! As far as losing our house, we weren't near there but we did have financial difficulties as where Bob worked the owners sold the business. Bob had worked there for 28 years. So everyone was leaving or getting fired. Bob then got the Assistant Service Manager at another dealership called Gordon Chevrolet. Which he had to start at half the pay he was getting. In the meantime I have problems where I worked and I blame most of them all on Nicole as she would call me crying all the time and I had to deal with that. Also, I think the impact of my son dying was also some of the problem. Anyways the State of Florida granted me a deal that I could not refuse. Now mind you that I worked for the state for almost 19 years with all but one being exemplary. I got raises when other people couldn't. I put my all into the job as I really liked it. I went above and beyond helping other people when they needed it without being told, etc. But at the end working under another boss that didn't like me she would never say I did anything good.

It was a he said she said type of problem. So they told me either to take the deal or get fired. So I terminated my employment so I could keep my benefits.

But it also decreased my pay by half. So yes, we had to make some adjustments.

Nicole with her lie about having to bail us out was just another one of her lies to make her look good. But not once did they offer to help us. I wouldn't have taken it anyways. Hine sight now I wished I would have.

It made Bob really mad that she would spread such a rumor. But that is what she did naturally, LIE!!!! That she sold Jason's house so that we could keep ours.

Chapter 4

They got their things and moved in a hotel near Busch Gardens with the kids. They were living it up buying, going places and doing drugs.

I kept looking for a home for them before they spent the money up. I finally found a mobile home on that side of town that was really nice for $17,000 in a nice park. I took Nicole over there and she also liked it. So we talked to the office and filled out all the papers. They set up a closing date for us to finalize things and then she could get the kids out of that motel room and have their own rooms.

The morning of the closing I picked Nicole and the kids up as Lee would hardly ever watch them as he was always going off with his friends. We were heading towards the park and Nicole started crying her crocodile tears stating that the bank had garnished her money due to a bill she owed University Community Hospital. At first I kind of believed her because when my kids were younger Nicole had to go in the hospital there. She would just lay there and cry. She was a little baby and they wouldn't put an IV in her and we threatened to take her out of the hospital if they didn't put one in her. They had all kinds of specialists in, thinking maybe she had rheumatoid arthritis or something like that as she favored her joints. She had been in there for about 3 days with no improvement and they said her veins were shallow that they would have to put the IV in her head and I said I didn't care. Just do it. Well they found another place to put it and after that she started getting better. They claimed she had Kawasaki Disease. To this day I am not sure what that is about. As when she left she was fine. I even had to take a note into my work as the boss didn't believe me when I told him that as he also had never heard of it either.

As her dad and I were divorced, they could not find him but found me and garnished my wages. I had to go down and prove I was the head of the household so that they would not garnish my wages. They said it didn't matter that her father's name was on the bill as I was her mother. I did have to make a payment schedule with them to pay them and the only reason I didn't was because I never received child support working two jobs and barely making it with my two kids. So since it happened to me I kind of thought it could be possible.

Well I took her to University Hospital to talk to them and explain that she was the head of the household in which we were told that they never did that. So therefore, she really made me mad lying. Next we went to her bank and she stated she would go in and see what the problem was. I said no I will go with you as I knew she was lying. They had spent all the money except for probably a few hundred dollars, which I made her give to me. I was furious as she ran me around knowing that there was no money left and we were supposed to be closing on this home. She did that to me without any guilt or remorse. I called Bob, he said go ahead to the closing to get the home. So there went my $15,000 plus. Bob also paid a year's lot rent so they only had to pay the electric, trying to make it easy for them to get back on their feet.

They moved in and shortly after Nicole kicked Lee out finally for the last time. She got a job at a trucking supply business and befriended a lady named Michelle. Nicole at this point was about 25 and Michelle had a son, Mark who was 19 which she wanted Nicole to meet.

They met and began to be very close which made Michelle happy. She and the kids eventually moved into Michelle's apartment stating that there was something wrong with the electric in the trailer. At this time I was trying to stay my distance from her as I was still really mad because we gave up our money I deserved and then some. Michelle was divorced and Mark usually stayed with his father but always came and visited Nicole. Mark had a sister in school that Nicole helped Michelle with, like picking her up from school, taking her places.

Michelle's divorced happened after her husband had brought a friend that he worked with home who didn't have a place to live and he moved in there helping with rent. Michelle eventually got involved with this man and then divorced Mark's dad. The kids were really mad. So Michelle could never let the kids see them together as it would really upset them. So in turn for Nicole staying at Michelle's the other benefit was that she could use Nicole's trailer to spend time with her boyfriend without worry. Nicole claimed that some of the electric worked but not the heater, refrigerator, I guess the big things. It was winter when Michelle invited Nicole to stay as she didn't want the kids to get sick and the arrangement was perfect for her.

Nicole had to renew her license so she talked me into taking her as they were expired, plus the fact that I wanted to see my babies. On the way back I asked her, now you have your license, do you have car insurance? She swore that she did. I was mad but I would have gone to the insurance place and paid for her a few months so she could build up and pay on her own. But she reassured me that she had insurance, another unnecessary lie.

Mark and Nicole were now just being friends. Maybe the age difference, her already having two kids and he was young. But they were good friends as he introduced her to some of his other friends.

The age difference bothered me some but I felt it would help her get over Lee even better which it did.

Chapter 5

Nicole was always on the go taking the kids with her and she had a real problem with Lee Lee sitting in his car seat. Even when I would take them he would get out and I would have to pull over and make him get in it.

One day she came over and she was going back to Michelle's apartment and Lee Lee had his seat belt off of the car seat and I made the statement to her to make sure he was in his car seat buckled in.

I guess probably an hour had passed and I received a call from her hysterically crying stating that they had just been in an accident. She stated that Lee Lee hit his head and it was the size of a basketball and they were taking him by helicopter to University Community Hospital. I was already in the car heading there and she called back and said they were now taking him to Tampa General Hospital. I arrived just before they brought him in. His head had gone down but he was unconscious. Brianna had her seat belt on so she didn't get hurt. It was not Nicole's fault as a lady had hit her. They brought Nicole in with Brianna and Nicole's arm was broken pretty bad. I guess the airbag did it.

I called the grandparents up in Alabama and they got the first plane down here. It seemed like they got here in a matter of a few hours. I was sitting in the ER with Nicole when Lee came in and said I get half of that money, first words out of his mouth. That is the kind of person he is. He didn't even ask how she was or hello, nothing. I was very disgusted.

The doctor came and told Nicole that they didn't know if Lee Lee would make it or not and he would be staying in the hospital for about 2 months if he lived. Well he made it but had serious brain damage, as he was not in his car seat and he went flying hitting the door a couple of times with his head.

There was a lot of tension in the waiting room as Lee was living with this girl which brought him to the hospital and stayed with him a lot. But she had a job and a little girl also. So she went home a lot. Nicole would not leave the hospital and I was there almost all of the time at first also, along with the grandparents from Alabama. Also his real father and his wife and two children came down.

All of Lee and Nicole's friends came on and off, some staying a long period of time.

We could go back and see Lee Lee only for short periods. It was sad as he had all kinds of tubes in him and he looked pitiful. You weren't allowed to say anything in the room or touch him. You just could stay and look at him. They wanted him to have quiet time as he was just put in there.

Friends would want to see him but either the parents or grandparents had to take them back to see him.

It was late and Michelle came up and wanted to see Lee Lee and everyone was really exhausted so I said I would take her back but she needed to be quiet and not touch him. We get in the room and he made a noise and she started talking to him maybe even touching him. I told her to stop and she wouldn't so I ran to the nurse's station and they said just what I told her so I said she is not listening. I was furious. The nurse got her out and I was so mad with her she didn't come back to see him for a long time.

Well everyone thought that she was coming into money. So it was going around that Michelle wanted money from Nicole as she stayed at her apartment and didn't pay rent. One day we went down stairs and Mark, Michelle's son still was very good friends with Nicole and was at the hospital a lot for her. We all sat around the table and I said I heard your mom said Nicole owed her money. I turned to Mark and told him to tell his mother that she got her rent when she was using Nicole's trailer to have her little rendezvous with her boyfriend. He really got angry as this was the man that broke her and his father up. So that is why Michelle had to hide it, not to upset her 2 kids.

I don't exactly remember how long he was in ICU but it was weeks. The grandparents stayed for a few weeks then they had to get back as Mr. Batts had leukemia and needed to get back home. By that time we had been told he would make it but would have brain damage.

I was keeping Brianna with us and Nicole's friend, Ashley also took Brianna a lot as she loved her so much. Always taking her shopping, buying her things and taking her places.

I noticed one day she had lice in her hair. She always had trouble with it. I treated it as well as Nicole did but this time it was really bad. Even when she would spend the night with Ashley as she lived with her parents she also was treating her for lice. As school was almost over Nicole talked to her teacher, whom said she was a really good student, not to worry. I took her to the school where she picked up all her stuff and the teacher told me to buy some books for her grade level and make her do some everyday, that they would pass her as it was so near the end of school. I asked the lady in the office about what do they recommend for lice as we have done everything but she kept getting them back. So she gave me a bottle of some solution she said she bought at the flea market, which I was very grateful for. She said it is the only thing she could find that really got rid of them.

After leaving the school I went back up to the hospital and outside where people would be smoking I treated Brianna's hair with the solution. They all looked as I know they knew what I was doing. But it did work finally. I had to go home and clean and wash everything before we could lay on the bed, couch, etc.

They finally put him in a regular room and began teaching him how to do everything over that he ever learned. They said he was lucky because he was so young, 4 years old.

Well little did we know that Lee Lee also had lice? That baby stayed in ICU for about a month and when he got to his regular room a few days later they discovered he had lice also. All that time he laid there with lice in his hair making him have an itchy head and could do nothing about it. We immediately shaved his head so there would be no more problems.

Everyone started to worry about her electric in the trailer as she said there was something wrong with it. We all wanted it fixed especially when she was going to bring Lee Lee home. While at the hospital one of their friend's sister worked at the electric company who talked her into going by and checking the electric out. Well come to find out she never paid the electric bill, so of course they turned it off. Yes there were some little things that would work as the park has to leave it on to show new tenants homes and may need to do some work on one of them. So I believe they leave something like 110 units on, so again another lie. I would have been embarrassed but not her; she has no guilt or shame.

He was in the room for about a month while they were trying to rehabilitate him and when he was to leave he would have to come back and get 3 different types of therapy 3 times per week.

At that point I called a lawyer for Nicole as it was not her fault but she lied to me again. She had no insurance, so the attorney said she would get nothing. The lady that hit her had insurance but had the minimum and had nothing to take or put a lien on. Lee heard about this and he called his own attorney, which must have stated the same thing. Lee like Nicole never left the hospital, till Lee heard there was not going to be any money. He then left but made visits when he could get his girlfriend to bring him up there. Now what kind of person is that? A sickening one, I think.

Towards the end before he got out he could be taken out for a few hours a day. We decided Nicole and the kids would move in with us as she had no car and I had to get him to therapy. She also decided to sell the trailer. So here again good ole mom stepped up and went and cleaned the whole trailer by myself. She never really even unpacked too much from when she first moved in. So I made a bunch of trips over to pick up everything. Once I moved all of the stuff out I told the lady in the park office that we wanted to sell it.

In the meantime, I went home and went through every bag and box there were, which was still ridden with roaches. So I just brought them to our house that didn't have roaches at all. I went through everything and I set up the bedroom for them when Lee Lee would get out. I had twin beds so Nicole could sleep with Lee Lee as they put the fear of God in me before we took him home stating that if he were to hit his head again it could be fatal. He had to wear a helmet for quite a while.

But while I was moving and wearing myself out she was taking Lee Lee and Brianna out with her friends and I don't believe watching him that well. Nicole always told Brianna to watch her brother. Plus the fact, I had to move her stuff all by myself while she was out playing. She could of just very well came to the house and helped me go through the stuff but instead she took him out sometimes way too long as he had to take medications. So once again, she could have cared less that I had to do that all on my own. She always screwed me over and didn't think a thing of it.

Also, at that time before Jason passed away I found out I had avascular necrosis and I had to have my hips replaced. I had one done before he passed and really thought hard whether I was going to get the other one done as I had to wait about 6 months before they would do the other hip and it was such a horrible experience.

I still wasn't walking very well so I went ahead and let them replace my other hip now having bilateral hip replacements. It did make me walk better but I still would have pain now and again. That also is one reason I was mad at Nicole as she knew I was running to the hospital every day and cleaning out her mobile home while she was hanging out with these much younger kids.

Chapter 6

While in the hospital she befriended this girl named Lisa who was married and also had 2 kids. I believe she was Lee's girlfriend's friend. She was at the hospital just about every day hanging with Nicole.

Well it finally came to the point that they were going to release Lee Lee and we were given strict instructions on what to do for him and to make sure he was at his therapy sessions three times per week.

Before they were to let him out Sheila, Lee's mother decided she wanted to come down then. I asked her please to give me a couple of weeks as I was so exhausted doing and running everywhere. Even the other grandparents told her to give me a break as I needed one.

Well the morning Lee Lee was to get out the phone rang in his room and it was Sheila. She stated that she was in a hotel on Dale Mabry Highway in Tampa. I was livid. So we get our orders and the hospital gave Lee Lee a really nice car seat. We packed in my new little SUV, Lee Lee very secured and I decided we would go by the hotel and let her see the kids. That is what we did.

We walked in and the first thing I saw was a little stuffed teddy bear with a big penis as large as the little bear was. She was what I called a cyber whore as she would meet these men on the internet and with the webcam I guess had been doing some kinds of sexual things that they watched each other. Well the man must have wanted her to come then as he paid for her gas and first night at the hotel. I really don't know if the bear was for him or if he gave it to her. Never saw anything like that before. She grabbed it up before the kids saw it and made some remark about it.

She had bought the kids a few things and we stayed for a little while. Then I decided to let her come to the house and see that I had nowhere for her to stay as the living room was still full of Nicole's stuff that I went through and had put in boxes which took most of the living room up. The other room was full with the beds and the kid's stuff. That is another reason I wanted her to wait. She should have come when everyone else was there. The grandparents told me not to let her drive with any of the kids in the car with her as she takes drugs that make her fall asleep and they were worried she might get in a wreck with them in her car.

In the hotel room she seemed fine. She seemed very alert and ready to go to my house. I told her to just follow me and we also let Brianna ride with her as she wanted her to and she did seem alright. Well we pull onto Dale Mabry and hit the first light. All of a sudden I feel someone run into the back of us. It was Sheila. I was furious as I had not even gotten Lee Lee home yet. Paramedics were called and since he had his helmet on and was really secured in the seat he didn't get harmed. The paramedics played with him for a little bit to make sure he was alright. In the meantime, we get Brianna from her and I started screaming at her. She said calm down she had insurance. That wasn't the point.

First I had just gotten this new SUV and she hit us as we were just taking Lee Lee home. The cops were called and she gave her information and they got mine, but I would not talk with her. I wanted her away from me. I was not taking her to my house then. I didn't care if she didn't have a place to stay. She should have listened to everyone and gave me some time. We were right in front of a car dealership so they just towed my SUV in their body shop as the SUV wasn't drivable. I called Bob at work and told him what happened, so we went in the showroom there after giving the body shop my information and waited for Bob to come and pick us up.

Brianna told us that she fell asleep and I felt really bad that we put her in the car with Sheila after the grandparents warned us about that.

Bob came and took us home, in the meantime her insurance company told me where to go pick up a rental till my SUV was fixed. I had to have a car because Lee Lee had to go to his therapy as they were trying to teach him to talk, walk and other things.

After that I would not let Sheila come over to our house as I was so mad. So she called Nicole where she had the kids with her over at the young teenager's house hanging out. Sheila called there and said she wanted to see them before she left, so she drove to where Nicole was with the kids. We had to pick Nicole up and the kids up, as it was late and very far from our home. Sheila got there just a little before Bob arrived to take them home. She was mad as she didn't get to see them that long. Finally the next day she left to go back to Alabama.

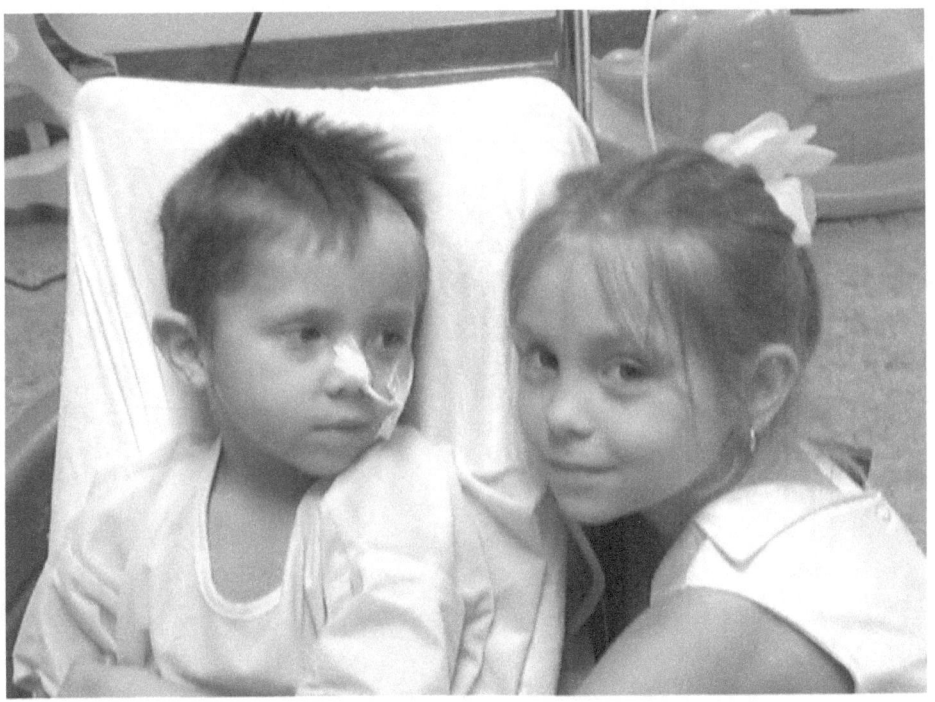

This is a picture of my 2 grandchildren when Lee Lee was in the hospital

This is a picture of my daughter with her two kids
while Lee Lee was in the hospital

This is a picture of my daughter

Chapter 7

After Sheila had left I was just so overwhelmed I had a nervous breakdown, overdosing on my medications and Benadryl. Well I ended up in Cardiac ICU for 2 days then was Baker Acted. While there I talked about all that I had been through and they changed my medications. They told me that I needed to stay away from Nicole as she was not helping me but putting me over the edge. In fact if she were still living with us I could not have gone home.

Her things were at the house but she did not stay there much especially after that. Bob told her but she was not at all concerned what I had done. Just thought I was stupid, which in a sense I was but I just couldn't handle anything else that might have come my way. It was the 4th of July weekend and they were letting a lot of us out and I felt so good to be able to first get some rest and talk about what had happened. My roommate was a doctor and the lady across the hall was a millionaire, which there were about 5 of us that really got along well. We were having so much fun at the end we all got told to be quite a few times.

I was scared when I first went in but found out that anyone could do this because of different reasons. Mine was Nicole. The doctor even stated that when she was always making Brianna watch Lee Lee that Brianna would also have problems as she wasn't giving her a chance to be a kid as she had to mother Lee Lee.

One night we were eating and the doorbell rang. It was the Dept. of Children and Family Services. Sheila went back home and tried to get us in trouble. She had pictures of the house I gave to Nicole which I stated was condemned. She must have taken pictures of all the broken glass on the side of the house and the roaches. Well when the lady walked in she acted really surprised as our house was still cluttered with Nicole's stuff in the living room but it was clean. She said you are supposed to have a lot of cats, which I said yes I did but she said I don't smell anything. That is because I keep them well maintained. I wouldn't have them unless I wasn't doing that. So she didn't really see anything that Sheila showed them pictures of up there. But she also stated that Nicole and I did drugs in front of the kids. WRONG!! We had to go and take a drug test which again made me really mad but we did it. A couple of days later the case was dropped. I wanted to press charges because that is a Federal offense but I didn't as the lady talked me out of it. Sheila must have confessed before she got caught up in her lie. So again, Sheila was just as bad as Nicole causing me so many problems.

The step grandmother, Maureen, was very upset that Sheila hadn't listened to me or them, telling her to give me a little time before she came down. Sheila had gotten custody of her two grandchildren from Jeremy as their mother was doing so many drugs during the last baby he was born and in a coma like state for quite a while as they found so many drugs in his little body. Well Sheila was granted custody of them as their father more or less like his brother Lee, just not violent. So Social Workers would come every so often to check on her with the kids. They always gave her advanced warning so on those days she would have everything clean and the boys there with her.

So Maureen had said she was always high and the kids were always filthy. So I believe she called up Dept. of Human Resources whom was the ones that always gave her advance notice that they were coming and told them to make an unexpected trip without telling her.

They did and Sheila was so high, she didn't know where the boys were and they drug tested her on the spot and took the boys away from her. She was so upset that she called Bob as I was still in the hospital thinking I turned her in. Bob told her that he didn't care what went on up there and that I was in the hospital so it was not us. She then thought it was Lee, but said he didn't have that much brains.

The boy's mother had been going through rehab and working hard to straighten out her life and the boys were given back to their mom.

Nicole was still running around with Lisa and the teenage kids. I think she thought since she was there I would babysit while she ran around. That was not happening especially then. So one morning my grandchildren came in and woke me up as I had my door closed. I led Brianna out of my room by her arm with Lee Lee following to where her mother was so she could watch them.

All she would do was talk 24/7 on the phone with these teenage kids and Lisa. One other day I walked out of my bedroom and she was on the porch talking on the phone with her back to Lee Lee which was outside the porch. He was getting in the above ground pool and she didn't even know it. I yelled at her to watch him and get him in the house.

Again, we could not get along as she wanted to be out partying and I wasn't going to have that in my house when she should have been a good mother and taking care of her kids instead.

Well she didn't like my rules so her and the kids moved in with Lisa, her kids, her sister and her mother. Lisa ended up taking Lee Lee to his therapy sessions and Nicole just using her up. I would occasionally watch them for her and every time they came over they were hungry. We would ask what they had to eat and said potato chips. Every time they came they were hungry. I went over there one day to pick up the kids and saw her mother drive up in an old pickup truck. She was very nice. They had kittens they had just put outside which I thought they were too young and this beige kitten caught my eye. I asked if I could have him and her sister said that was her favorite one but she let me have him.

So I left and talked to Nicole once in a while. She started coming by the house in this new used car. I asked her whose car was that and she stated it was Lisa's mom's new car. I thought why would this lady be driving an old pickup and letting Nicole have her car, didn't make sense. So after a while I always kept in touch with Ashley and her family and Ashley told me she had sold the trailer. Ashley said she didn't tell us as she knew we wanted some of the money back we laid out for her and she wasn't going to give us any. So the lie about the car was another guiltless selfish act. When she moved in Lisa's home she met this guy who had lived in New Port Richey. He seemed to like Nicole pretty well even bringing his son to see her.

She had to move from Lisa's as they could not afford them living there and since she now had a car she also moved in an apartment in New Port Richey to be near this guy. She had bought herself a bedroom suit and the kids slept on the floor. She should have been the one on the floor not her kids.

Well again she was getting in all kinds of trouble and we bailed her out of jail costing us $200 as her bail was $2,000 for the Driving While License Suspended With Knowledge. About a week later I get a call on the phone from Nicole she was crying and stating that she was going to harm herself and tell the kids she loved them. I am in a panic as I rushed out the door in rush hour traffic to get from Tampa to New Port Richey. I finally arrived and it was a gated community. I saw her talking to the Sheriff Officer and she would not let me in that gate until the she told the Officer of her story. Then finally she let me in. I was so upset as the Officer said that she was just mad and she (the Officer) was not going to take her anywhere. I was angry as I had just drove over an hour and they wouldn't let me in at first and then this. I was getting mad with the Officer and finally I said take me then. She said no she wouldn't do that. But before I left I told her of the bond we paid for her. She told me to go the bondsman that night and get it revoked, which I did. It cost us another $300 but later that night Mr. Batts came through for Nicole and the bond was still good as they had to pay the whole $2,000. Well guess what, she missed her Court date and they lost their money. But to her she could have cared less. I'm just glad we did revoke it or it would have been us out of another $2,000 which we didn't have.

So we decided we were going to sell our house and move into this 55+ community so I knew she could never come and live with us, hopefully getting away from her some. As I said she used me up. Her problems were my problems. So our house sold and we found a nice mobile home and doing great.

After a little while, she found out that the guy she was having a relationship with was married so they were no longer intimate friends. She met another guy while driving to the store that pulled up beside her and asked her for her number. So they started talking. He liked to ride the crouch rocket bikes and could do a lot of tricks and stuff with it. They were together for a little while but I really don't know what happened with that situation.

Because the next thing I found out that she was living with this couple in their home. I guess she ran out of money and moved in with them.

She hardly knew these people, Dan and Karen, and I guess they got mad with her as I'm sure she was not contributing anything and they told her to get out but she could leave the kids. WHAT A MISTAKE!!!!

I talked to her a few times and then I found out the kids were staying with this couple and she told me where so I went over to the house to see them. I learned that they were abusing them. Now remember Lee Lee had been out of the hospital only a few months and when they punished him they would put him in their dog's crate as they had a big dog. Also, they made him go to bed earlier and I asked Brianna how he goes to sleep in her living room floor with all the noise. She told me that they gave him medicine to sleep. Brianna also later told us that they would put him in a corner and make him hold his arms up for long periods of time. The day I was there when I was leaving she had let her dog out and he pooped in the neighbor's yard. When I was leaving he came out and started yelling at Karen. She turned around and told Brianna to pick it up and she started crying as she was tiny for her age and it was a big dog. I told Brianna to get me something and I cleaned it up.

The next morning the girl called and said Brianna wouldn't walk to school alone as she was scared. I was so mad at Nicole for leaving them there. I talked to her and told her I was going to be picking up the kids as Karen also watched her sister's little boy that was still in diapers. She made Brianna her servant having to clean, do dishes, change diapers and remember she was just 7. I found out later that she would leave for long periods of time and left Brianna in charge.

So the next morning I got up really early and went over and knocked on her door and said I was there to pick them up. She said that was not the plan, I don't know what that meant but she gave them to me with nothing but the clothes on their back. She kept their clothes. I don't know if that was spite or what.

So here I took them home with me to a 55+ community knowing I couldn't keep them for long. Nicole made no effort to get them. All she wanted to do was party and have fun with her friends.

She called one day to say that she was going to start dancing I guess she thought we would give her money so she wouldn't do that. Well by that time we didn't have much money and I said do what you have to do. She could have gotten a job elsewhere as she did graduate from high school. I guess one of her friends was dancing so she started dancing too. I really wasn't worried about her as she could have cared less what happened to her kids or us.

Chapter 8

As soon as Ashley heard I had Brianna, she said I want to keep her as she did know we couldn't for long. As she lived with her parents, she had to ask them first. They took Brianna in with open arms. She could not have been in a better place. As I said Ashley loved Brianna. All her mother said that she needed to help her with Brianna. Ashley was a few years younger than Nicole so she still liked to go out and her parents would watch Brianna. They made her up her own room. They were so nice to her. On the weekends we would keep her to give them a break as I knew I could probably get away with that where we lived. Plus the fact we got to spend our time with her and she could also see her brother while he was here.

We still had Lee Lee which we kept him for about 3 months until someone told on us. We were Faith Riders then, riding our motorcycle for the Lord at Idlewild Baptist Church. Every week there was a prayer list going around in our class and every week we put Nicole on it. So every weekend we would take them to church with us. They enjoyed it as much as we did.

I wished I had known she could just leave her kids as I would have done things different such as staying where we lived so we could keep them.

But after they found out we had to send Lee Lee up to Alabama to live with his father as he had gone back months earlier as he had used everyone up down here.

When Lee got there he first stayed with his mother, Sheila, and one night Lee went out and got severely beaten by about 3 guys. They said it was by the police as Maureen's brother was an Officer up there somewhere. He was so badly beaten his ear was almost torn off. They begged him to go to the hospital and he said no because that is what he deserved for doing it to Nicole all that time.

He moved in with his grandparents, which I knew if his grandfather was around the kids would be fine. He was such a gentleman. Lee even told us he had a job and was going to church.

Ashley still had Brianna down here. She stayed with Ashley and her family for about 8 months before they had to send her back as Ashley started lacking in helping her mother plus the fact no one was helping them financially with Brianna. Ashley I think to this day blames herself for Brianna getting sent back which she should never think that as it was not her responsibility. Nicole talked to her I think twice at Ashley's house and we made an effort a couple of times on the weekends to get Nicole so she could spend time with the kids. If we didn't do that she would have never saw them and I guess really didn't matter.

Chapter 9

We had made arrangements for Lee to pick up Brianna as we didn't have a place yet to keep her. Since Mr. Batts was still alive I knew the kids would be in good hands.

Lee finally lost his job due to smoking pot and they had drug tested him. He also lied about going to church, I believe, because after a few months Mr. Batts passed away from Leukemia.

That is when all hell broke loose, which I knew it would.

Nicole at that time was living with this guy named Ray. She was still dancing and he was a drug dealer. He had two little boys that Nicole spent her time with as Ray did pay child support and the kids were often over at his house. She was like a second mom to them. Bizarre, as she could of cared less about her own.

Nicole at this point started to get in trouble with the law, getting tickets for driving with license suspended while knowing.

She kept avoiding paying her tickets and they mounted up.

She told us that she worked for a gym and one night I was trying to find her and they said she never worked there she was a customer. Also, another diner she supposedly worked at Three Coins and also when I called they also didn't know her. I guess she didn't want me knowing that she was still dancing.

She was put in the Pinellas County Jail a few times due to these tickets she was accumulating. I went to see her and even had to pick up her boyfriend Ray as he didn't have a license either.

After Mr. Batts funeral Lee stayed with the kids at Maureen's house. Lee got them taken away from him a few times due to drugs and domestic violence.

The kids were actually given to Carl and Tara Copeland who already had 3 kids of their own. But they were not Carl's kids. The kid's father was in prison.

Lee had to go through some classes and different things and eventually got the kids back.

He found a girlfriend up there named Pam. She was 21 and had 5 kids all taken from her. So therefore she really wasn't allowed to be around Brianna or Lee Lee.

Lee was not working and still living with Maureen and moved Pam in with him. He beat her badly all of the time.

Nicole got a subpoena to be in Court in Fayette County, AL. Bob and I gave her the money to go and when she got there; there was nothing but trouble. He was trying to put the moves on Nicole as usual but Nicole had no interest in him anymore. While there he also beat Pam a few times. One breaking her nose which Maureen said she did it to save his butt. But Maureen is very little and Pam was very tall so no one believed that she had done it. Nicole saw it and said Lee did it.

They went to court and Lee gave his rights up from the kids so he would not have to pay child support and Nicole stated that she was not giving up her rights. She was to come back and get a home for them so the Social Worker could come out and verify that she did have a place, food, and clothing for them.

Every time they tried to get ahold of her she was never around so the kids stayed in Alabama.

While Mr. Batts was alive they went and applied for Public Assistant and he got an apartment for him and the kids to stay in. So they all had their own bedroom.

Lee was getting in trouble because of him beating Pam up so much. In one week he put her in the hospital 3 times and then they put his picture in the newspaper because of it. My poor granddaughter had to go to school with all the kids and you know how kids can be cruel.

Brianna ended up having to have her tonsils out. So after she got out they thought it best for her to recover at Carl and Tara's house as there was always something that was going on at Lee's apartment. Lee Lee stayed with dad and continued catching the bus going to school. He had to ride a handicap bus due to his brain injury so when Brianna was living there before her surgery she rode the same bus with him so he wouldn't feel bad. She was such a good big sister.

One day Lee and Pam were in the apartment when the Social Worker stopped by to see how things were going. They were high so they would not answer the door. In the meantime, Lee Lee got off the school bus and went to the door which was locked and knocked and knocked; they wouldn't let him in as the Social Worker was still out there. So Lee Lee went next door when they decided to take him away from Lee again. So they took Lee Lee to Carl and Tara's home, as they seemed more responsible. When Pam was there and the Social Worker would come she always went out the bathroom window. But this time was Lee's final chance at keeping them. As his violence and bad behavior, they were not letting him be around the kids unsupervised.

Chapter 10

Well by this time I was calling the Department of Human Resources (DHR) and asking them why the kids were given to people that they really didn't know and non-related.

I told them I was the maternal grandmother and I was next in line to get them.

In the meantime, Bob and I decided to buy a house so we could get out of the 55+ community and have the kids with us.

That was not an easy task. We looked at over 100's of homes by ourselves then got hooked up with this one mortgage company that ran us around for 7 months. The broker actually was trying to put us in a home we could not afford and with that we paid almost $1,000 in inspections, etc. So since we didn't get the house we lost about $1,000.

Nicole was still out there at the strip clubs doing her thing and getting into more trouble. Not worried at all about her kids. She would call now and again but it usually was when she had gotten into trouble.

Well after 7 months of hell with this mortgage company, we finally changed to another company, which I didn't know we could have. Getting financed was a horrible experience. They want to interrogate you to the hilt. So the next company after 2 months of pure hell again, we finally got our home.

I started writing to the Governor in our state and in Alabama, also, sent a copy to President Obama. They had all replied but stated we needed an attorney. I kept asking why when I was the one to get them as I was the maternal grandmother. I was told that Lee could give them to whomever he wanted. I said he gave his rights away, how could that be. I never ever got any response back from DHR. Nor any help but to tell me to get an attorney.

Since we spent so much money getting into this house and going through hell, thinking Nicole was going to be part of their lives I couldn't afford an attorney. It was horrible.

One day I sat in front of Publix Supermarket with a Petition to try to get my grandkids back. I got over 200 signatures and was still going to proceed getting more. I was told that this was not that kind of case that a petition would not do anything for me. Well it did for me as everyone that came by signed it as they thought Alabama was wrong in not letting us have them to begin with. I had checked the schools out here and found out they had a special program for Lee Lee. I fought for about a year before I really gave up.

Carl and Tara had gotten a divorce so she took her kids with her and left Brianna and Lee Lee with Carl who had a liver transplant and not doing well. He went to work but after school the kids would be alone for a few hours a day which I didn't think it was appropriate at least not for Lee Lee as he needed special care. So I complained about that and then Carl would not let me talk to them anymore.

For one reason Lee's brother was put in prison for molesting a little girl about Brianna's age and when he got out he was living near that town knowing they were home alone. Don't know if anything would have happened but it was his step-daughter he had molested. So that was always in the back of my head. As Lee Lee didn't know any better but to open the door if someone came.

Carl whom was left with the kids was getting very sick with his liver transplant wasn't doing well.

So the next time I find out that Carl just gave them to a preacher and his wife which again my grandkids didn't know. I was upset as he knew I was trying to get them and he just overlooked me as Sheila and Maureen filled his head with who knows what. They too lied a lot.

I just don't understand how that can happen!!!

Chapter 11

In the meantime, Nicole is still dancing and doing her drugs. At this time she was dancing in Clearwater where she met this man which was quite a few years older, in his early 40's, named Jim and she was only 26.

He was from North Carolina, a well polish business man. He was in love with Nicole. His work took him to Florida and Texas that I know of. While in Florida he worked at Orlando, but always managed to make his way to Clearwater every time he was here.

This man bought her a diamond tennis bracelet, ring, name brand purse, and always gave her money. He put her in a really nice apartment at first, even renting her furniture and paying for it for months in advanced. If she was out of money she would always call him and make up some lie. One time she told him that her dad had died and her and I went up there but had no money to get back so she wanted him to send her money. Her father wasn't dead. In this apartment she got robbed. I guess also she didn't pay the rent like she was supposed to and he rented her another apartment.

He told us that she would make him drive her to these houses and wait in the car and would want quite a bit of money. He either didn't want to believe it or just overlooked it as when he told me I said she was in there buying drugs.

In total, he put her in 3 different apartments. The last she never even stayed in. We had helped her find the apartment and moved the kid's beds, clothes, and toys in it.

My friend had bought both of the kid's new air mattresses and bedding for them plus clothes as she needed to show the Social Workers she had a place and things for them to stay with her.

Well I hadn't heard from her for a while so we went over to the apartments where we had met the couple next door when we moved her in as this was a duplex. Of course we got there and no one would answer the door because no one was there. We were about to leave and the neighbors pulled up and was in total shock. Nicole had told them I got shot in the head and was at Tampa General Hospital fighting for my life. Another lie!!!! They were relieved to see me but said Nicole never even stayed there.

After a while when Jim would come down to see her she would avoid him.

So he called me one day, and I found out more than I wanted too. She used him up, actually spending about $17,000 in about 5 or 6 months. He said she still could of used him but for some reason she didn't want to see him anymore. At this point she was very hooked on the pills, Oxycodone or Roxicodone.

He finally got a hold of her talking to me every day for a couple of weeks just trying to think where her head was. We talked a lot and finally Nicole called him and apologized to him. He wanted to meet with her one last time, have dinner and talk. But she wouldn't give him the satisfaction. So he sent her a Bible, statute of a mother holding her baby and $100.

We went to meet her at Diamond Dolls where she was supposed to be working. When we pulled up she got in the car and I handed her the stuff. Her phone kept ringing the whole time while in the car. It was her knew found druggie boyfriend that lived in New Port Richey, FL. Finally we see this black guy, really filthy waiting at the corner of the building and I asked if that was her new boyfriend and she said no it was the bouncer of the club.

Come to find out she walked inside for a minute to act like she was going to work for our benefit, when she wasn't even allowed to be in that club anymore. I don't know what happened that she could not work there any longer, maybe the pills.

But we found out that this guy Reese that was waiting for her was her boyfriend and they both lived at his grandmother's home in New Port Richey where she was dancing again.

See he provided her a place to live and drugs, so she was set.

She even said they were going to church and one day while there they took the collection plate and just poured it over their heads while sitting there. I just couldn't believe that as I had never heard of such a thing, but again she was a pathological liar.

The police/sheriff must have been watching Reese for quite some time. He and this girl that worked at a doctor's office were writing bogus scripts.

One night Nicole called all upset and told us she got arrested as the girl she was with at the convenient store stole something and they checked Nicole's pockets and found some drugs.

Later on we learned the truth. She took one of those bogus prescriptions and tried to get it filled. Well she got caught and had to go to Court on it.

Reese and the nurse also got caught, but as they had been doing it for a long time and the police/sheriff had been watching them they got a 25 year sentence, at least that is what Nicole said they got. Since she was just involved in the last incident before they got caught they knew she hadn't been doing that for long so they arrested her. Someone posted bail for her that time, I don't know who did. But I know she had to go to Court on it.

Chapter 12

While dancing in New Port Richey she met a new guy, she is fatally in love with. He is not married but just as well should be as he and his so-called-wife has been together for about 17/18 years I heard. While Nicole was going to her Court appearances she was staying with us as we were providing her with the transportation. This new guy was named Craig. As far as everything else went he seemed to be a very good person. Nicole and he became the closest of friends. I thought at one time he would leave his "wife" but they fight too much now and he sees how she manipulates, lies and uses people. But when he was first calling here I picked up the phone and he said you are her step-mom, right? I was shocked that he said that as he proceeded to tell me that her mother had died.

I told him then he needed to come over one day without Nicole being here and let's have a talk. He came in, sat down and we were talking. He said I hope you don't think I look like that guy Reese and no way did he, very clean and buffed. I looked at him and said do I look like someone you know. He looked for a minute and said "No". I said I am Nicole's real mother and I didn't know why she had told him that. Now that makes 2 times I died and 1 for her dad which now is really dead.

Craig told us that she came into his work crying stating that I had died. He just couldn't believe it but she already had it set up as she told him that everyone says that her step-mom (me) looked similar to her.

All her Court appearances were coming up and she had to go to Court in 3 different counties.

She had to go to Pasco County also due to driving while license suspended while knowing and drugs.

We took her to Pasco County Court first where the Judge was trying to get her off the drugs through a rehab. She stayed in jail a few days before they could get her in one. Finally they found one for her in Auburndale, FL which was about a 2 or 3 hour drive from here.

When she had to go to Court we would have to drive there and take her to Court and drive back. It was getting old. So the last time we took her to Pinellas Court, they gave her time served and we were to take her back to the program. I didn't know no one else could bring her back so I mentioned could Craig do it as we were not too well then and wanted to get home.

So after he got off of work he took her back and instead of dropping her off down the street she let him drop her off right in front so everyone could see her new boyfriend and how cute and hunky he was.

Well she called us from there when she got back and said she got in trouble for him taking her back. I talked to someone there as I thought it was our fault not hers that time. But they wanted to kick her out, as if you ever broke any rule they didn't want you there. They wanted the ones they could help.

So that night she left, calling us from some payphone to come and get her. I told her she needed to go back and she said she couldn't so Craig went and picked her up and brought her here.

Now there was a warrant out due to her leaving the facility and not reporting it to the Court and was still dancing and doing her drugs.

She was staying here so we could transport her to Court. One night she was arguing with me about something and I said to her, "You just don't want your kids." All hell broke loose then as she was packing her things and cussing me the whole way out the door calling me a, mother-fucking bitch, and a whole lot of other obscenities.

So she called a cab and went to a hotel to stay while dancing.

She was working in Tampa, FL near Brandon dancing as they were making more money there.

One night on their way home as Craig used to always take her and pick her up, he was pulled over due to his expired tag. They asked for her ID and she showed them. Well she had a warrant in Pinellas County as she never made the Court date. So they took her to Orient Road Jail in Tampa. She had to stay there about a week as she also had those pending vehicle violations to take care of. Then she was transported to Pinellas County to go to Court for the bogus prescription as that happened in Clearwater.

When Craig picked her in the rehab in Auburndale the last day she was there is when her last appearance for Pinellas was as they gave her time served. Then they were going to transport her to Pasco where they had put her in the drug treatment facility and took off from there.

She was looking at doing some long time. So when her Court appearance came up Craig for the first time showed up in Court maybe thinking he knew she was going to be put away for a while.

The Judge offered her 328 days and 11 hours not making it a felony, although she had a felony record already from Pinellas about the prescription refill. She looked at us and we are telling her to take the deal because if she didn't she might have ended up going somewhere else or something.

Chapter 13

So now she is in jail and her stuff was still at the hotel room. Wow, I wonder who she called, me!!!!

I had to go to the office and tell them she was in jail but at first they would not give it to me.

The next day was a week day so I called the manager and she said yes come and get her things.

Bob wasn't feeling well so I went to pick up all this stuff. When I got there it was upstairs which I can't walk stairs really good due to my hips being replaced. When I walked in I couldn't believe all the stuff I had to move. I made about 8 trips and it started to rain so the maintenance man was kind enough to start helping me, as I was sobbing so hard then as I was hurting so badly. I got it all in the car and brought it home and put in our garage.

I set up appointments to visit with her every week. I thought maybe her being in there would give her a new outlook, ha-ha!!

She was earning extra time off by doing road crew. The Deputy out there saw that she was to herself and just did her work and started to get to know Nicole. Actually she would have Nicole train all the new road crew girls that would come out. Every week she seemed remorseful and saying she would never come back there because she had learned her lesson. Craig never went to see her the whole time she was in there. But he did put money on the phone so he could talk to her at any time she could use the phone. As sometimes when there were fights and such their phone privileges were lost.

Craig always made sure she had money for the canteen too. I know the man had to spend over $2,000 for the phone and canteen while she was in there.

Bob and I went to visit Nicole in jail every visiting day. We made plans that Nicole would come and live with us again. She would get a job and get her kids back. They would all live with us. She would have had a built in babysitter for as long as she stayed with us. She could save for a car, save money and eventually get a small place for her and the kids to live. There was even a possibility that Craig would help her out.

Well that never happened. The first thing Nicole did after being in jail and not smoking for almost a year, was to light up a cigarette in her first 5 minutes of freedom.

Bob was thinking to himself, could this be a sign of things to come. (It was!!), as none of our plans worked out.

Bob was Nicole's step-father but he felt responsible for her. He had told her to take off for a couple of weeks and relax, then look for a job.

After almost a month of lying around doing nothing but party and making no attempt to get her kids back, Nicole went back to dancing.

Bob thought she did that because the money was real good, and she could hire a lawyer to regain custody of her kids. He was wrong. Nicole wanted to get her own place so she wouldn't have to listen to my advice and she could play house with Craig.

The first thing Nicole did when she got paid was to get a cell phone. She was on that cell phone 24/7. She would be outside at 2:00 a.m. screaming and cursing at the top of her lungs.

I told her to cool it with the screaming and cursing because our neighbors were commenting on it.

But it kept on for the next eight months. You see Nicole does what ever she wants to do with absolutely no remorse.

I told Nicole that she needed to start paying us rent, as you don't live anywhere for free. That's something else Nicole never did. Nicole asked me, "Why should I have to pay rent?"

Bob figured after she lied to everyone about paying us $250 a week that maybe she could come up with $100 a week, but she couldn't.

She would tell us that it was slow in the clubs and she only made somewhere between $17.00 and $30 something near there a night. Another Lie!!!! She was spending her money on drugs.

That's right she was on the drugs again and the shit hit the fan. Her married boyfriend, Craig, broke it off with her because she was back on drugs. I was devastated. Nicole quit her dancing jobs at the strip clubs in order to keep off the drugs and mainly to get back with Craig.

She was out of work for another month, always with the story that she found a job but can't start for 2 or 3 weeks, another lie, there were no jobs.

She finally landed a job at a telemarketing company. We paid to have her cell phone turned back on so she could call us for rides, and we gave her lunch money because she didn't get paid for 2 weeks. Sounds like something you would do for a 15 year old not a 31 year old.

That is when Bob decided to keep track of the actual cash that we laid out for her and the money she paid back to us.

She worked at the telemarketing for about a month and then Craig made her quit because her boss was flirting with her, (so she said).

Here we go again another 3 weeks off. We turned her phone back on again to keep our phone from being monopolized.

I get Nicole a good job as a waitress at a real nice bar and grill. She meets new friends at work and starts dating one of the guys from work. She and Craig broke up and she was OK with that.

We thought this was great, she is out of that go no where situation with Craig.

Things were starting to look good.

Now Craig wants back in with Nicole. Bob asked; why would a married man with 3 kids that just bought a house want with Nicole (Must be in the booty calls).

He kept calling her phone but she wasn't answering it, so he comes to the house and I go to the door and told him she wasn't here. He snuck around to Nicole's bedroom window and heard Nicole and I talking. So he decides to call her cell phone and it rings in the room so he knew she was here. So I let him in and they talked.

They got back together and here we go again. They go out drinking real late at night, or the all night fighting and screaming on the phone.

The result is that Nicole cannot get up out of bed in the morning to be at work on time. Bad part is she could have cared less.

Bob told her, "If you're not interested in getting to work on time then maybe I am not interested in taking you." Her response was not, I'm sorry or I'll do better, but was "That's OK I'll get a ride."

It could have been Bob just getting tired of driving her to and from work. He is retired and couldn't do anything all day because he was Nicole's full time chauffeur.

It turns out that she didn't have to worry about a ride anymore because she got fired that day.

Bob dropped her off at work she didn't go inside as she was arguing on the phone with Craig as usual. She went and sat on the bench outside and talked on her cell phone. Her boss gave her a choice, go to work or go home. She called us for a ride and lied to us again.

She told us she got fired because she had started her period and needed to go home and change and the boss wouldn't let her go. He said if you go home you can stay home.

Bob had learned that when Nicole's stories don't make sense she is lying.

Again she is out of work for about another month. After a while of her not working, we all started getting on each others nerves. After all Nicole has been staying and mooching off us for almost 8 months now.

A big argument started between Nicole and me. Nicole freaks out, because she said she was paying us rent. All Bob could hear was Nicole yelling and cursing at me. Craig, Nicole and I were in Nicole's room, Bob comes in and says "Why is it that people think screaming and cursing makes them right?"

Nicole got angry and told Craig to take her out of here. Bob thought to himself, where is he going to take her? Certainly not home to his wife and 3 kids. Well they went for a ride and came back.

Nicole had given us some money from time to time, but it was not for rent. It was paying us back for the cash that we have laid out for her.

Nicole and Bob were not speaking at this time, so he wrote her a letter explaining that I kept records just for an occasion like this.

Here is a copy of the letter:

April 17, 2011

Dear Nicole,

Being that we are not talking I am writing this letter. It has come to my attention that you feel you have been paying us rent every week and you only missed a few times.

Are you starting to believe your own lies? Or, is it your way of not having to appreciate the room and board that we have provided?

You see I have kept a record of the actual cash that you have given us back since September of 2010. It is $603. If you deduct the cash that we have laid out for you:

Fed Ex for Brianna's dress, Your half of the kids Christmas, Turning your phone on twice

Your shoes and clothes for your waitress job; comes to $605.

I am not counting room and board or transportation. That means you still owe us $2 before you even start paying rent. In reality you have not paid any rent, room and board, food or gas for the last 34 weeks.

Sincerely,
Bob

Chapter 14

The next lie or act of deceit came when she told us she was going to the gym with Craig on a regular basis.

We noticed that she was gone on the same days and hours as when she was dancing. She was working, but didn't want us to know so she wouldn't have to pay us.

Things got very cold in the last week or so that Nicole lived with us.

She had borrowed my necklace I had made of my son, Jason. She put it back and everything was cool, but months later it turned up missing.

Naturally Nicole said she didn't have it but she would look for it. She didn't remember or didn't know right then where it was. I begged her to tell me if she pawned it so I could go get it as it was very special to me.

Nicole swore that she did not pawn it.

You see this necklace was very precious to me as it was a picture of my son. I sent off right after he passed away and had it made. It was etched into a charm on my 18kt gold necklace, which ended up being the value of $1,625.00.

An argument ensued and Nicole moved out with all of her possessions.

A few days later Bob was cleaning her room and guess what he found? It was the pawn slip for my necklace. Nicole had gotten $130.00 for it. The return date was expired and the necklace was no longer at the pawn shop.

Bob thought to himself you have to be a liar and a thief with absolutely no remorse to do something like that.

Craig took his family back to visit in New York where he is from and he came back earlier than his so called wife. She kept the 2 younger ones as the oldest had to go to summer school.

On the way back Craig breaks down and he called Nicole as he gave her $600 to hold for him. STUPID!!!!! Nicole talked to him and said she would meet his friend outside and give him the money. Well after that she would not answer her phone nor did the guy ever see her. I'm sure she had fun with his money. Maybe she thought he wouldn't need it right away, wrong!!!

So now Craig is stuck with his daughter at this auto shop in North Carolina and doesn't have the money to get it fixed. He and his daughter had to spend the night in a hotel and late the next day someone sent him money to come home on a bus.

So he called me to see if I had talked to her because he was stressing about the money and not getting ahold of her. So he called me on and off all that day. Even into the next day.

He gets home and the next morning I guess he goes out to try to find her. He goes to the club and they said they hadn't seen her. But he kept looking. Around 7:00 he called me and stated that he had some news. I told him Nicole had just called me and said she needed help and that she was willing to be Baker Acted. So when he did call I told him that we were on our way to pick her up to take her to the hospital.

He replies back, so you are leaving now it should take you all about 30 minutes to get here. He said she wouldn't open the door for him so I told him to wait outside and he could go in with us.

We get there and I see Craig's car. I'm knocking on the door and Nicole is saying wait a minute, which was about a 10 minute wait. I tried to mess with his car to get the alarm to go off but that didn't work. So when she finally opened the door I looked around for Craig and didn't see him but saw the bathroom door closed. I went straight there and opened the door as I was mad as he said he was going to wait on us. When I opened the door of the bathroom he was putting on his shirt, booty call!!! That also made me mad as he was so angry with her while talking to me and now he was over there having sex. I guess they ran over the 30 minutes he had anticipated. I started hitting him, not hard, and saying to him that he was a liar. Bob said Nicole was freaking out that I was doing that to him. My focus was on him as most of the week I was put through hell again because of the two of them.

She told us that she was embarrassed because she didn't have the money but took a whole lot of oxytocin and her roommate found her outside passed out on the ground and made her come in. She said she slept the whole time until she woke up when Craig kept knocking on her door.

So we take her to the hospital which she stayed until she was transported again to the Harbor. She stayed her 72 hours and we brought her back home when she got out. They had put her on 3 different kinds of medications. One was an antidepressant; one was for anxiety and the other for sleeping at night as she was still going through withdrawals.

When we picked her up she was like a whole different other person, I guess due to the medications. But yes, she stopped taking them while she was here, said she didn't need to take them at all.

She had follow up appointments for outpatient care and the first appointment we took her to was a major disaster.

I didn't know if I was going to be able to talk to the doctor so I wrote a note to let them know that she was not taking her medications and was behaving badly again.

We get there and she signed in and we all sat down, then she went to smoke a cigarette. I then went up to the window and handed the note to the guy that was taking care of the patients coming in and told him that her doctor needed to read this.

He said OK but he thought maybe I could go in with her. She had come back in and saw me put it down. So I went back to sit down and I see her go to the counter and reach over and grabbed it.

I was furious. I got up really fast and took a hold of her purse with one had and my other hand I was trying to grab for the letter. In the meantime she is screaming "don't hit me—don't hit me." I didn't even have a hand on her.

The guy must have thought she was cute or something because he never said one word to her but to me he stated that this could not happen in there.

So I quit and told Bob lets go. I hollered she is yours now because I can't be put through this anymore. So we get in the car and we leave her there. She went to her appointment and the doctor did read my letter. She found a way home and came in and asked if she could stay for 2 days. I was really reluctant but I said yes as the Social Worker said she couldn't stay at the hospital and that she was better off here.

Little did she know what Nicole had put us through for years? A day or two later the Social Worker made an appointment to meet with Nicole here. She called and stated that she was running late so we went to the store.

Next thing, I get a phone call from the Social Worker that she is at our house and Nicole had taken off. I told her we were on our way home to wait as we weren't far.

When we got home she came in and we explained most everything she has done to us in the past. That she was a pathological liar and had a narcissistic personality. We told her that my doctor had told me to stay away from her. So she suggested a program that would be 6 months to a year, I guess depending upon her progress. They would get her off the drugs and show her how to be responsible for herself. They would even get her a job. I said she would never go for it.

She said it was a red flag to her when she got there and Nicole took off with Craig stating she had to go to the store and would be right back, which took her at least 30 minutes. The Social Worker said there should have been nothing that she had to leave about due to her being there.

When she did finally arrive she came in with a big attitude. We all were sitting down at the table discussing things and she stood where the chair was and the Social Worker told her to sit down. She said, "No" and said you don't want me to live here which I said, "yes" while all the time she was standing she was in a fighting stance looking at me, like she wanted to come over the table at me. So she left with Craig which they later came back and got her stuff. The Social Worker said now that she is out of Hernando County into Pasco County she could not help her but she knew the Social Worker in Pasco and that she would give her a call.

We received quite a few messages on the answering machine stating that she missed her appointments.

I was still on her case to pay me back the money for the necklace. She said she was not making money here but the girls go down to Miami now and they make a lot of money down there. I think they stay for about a week at a time.

So Craig buys her a new cell phone as the night we went to take her to the hospital she stated that her phone ended up in the water. Who knows? He didn't want her down there with no phone. I talked to her a few times while she was down there and at first said she couldn't start until Monday which she had arrived that Friday.

Well I have been calling Nicole on and off as she was supposed to pay me $800 for my necklace she pawned. But that eventually became a multitude of lies. I threatened that I was going to press charges, which I am debating.

She stayed almost a week and Craig went to pick her up and his truck breaks down again. So she called me to tell me, and I asked her if she had my money and she said, "Yes".

So when they got back, I still didn't see my money. She stated that Craig wanted his money first as she owed him $600. When I asked Craig he told me she never gave him any money. So again, she strung me along for a couple of weeks, about this money. I called and said I was going to press charges on her to try to get her to make an attempt to pay me something. But I guess that all went to the sleazy hotel room she was staying in and drugs.

I was really counting on the money as we were in the hole with helping her out about that much and that would bring us up to date. I should have known better.

So again I was staying my distant. We do not want her living with us anymore because her last stay with us was uncomfortable.

She was getting scary. We caught her listening in on all of our phone calls. She would also pretend that she was me, if she answered the phone before we did.

She would ask our neighbors if she could borrow money. She would walk down to the shopping center and panhandle. She would grub for cigarettes and would even pick up cigarette butts that were lying in the street. Bob noticed her going into a fighting stance at the drop of a hat.

She is just using us. At 31 years of age, she wants her mother to a mom to her, but she doesn't want to be a mother to her own children.

Besides living with us would not be helping her. She needs professional help, not free room and board.

The Final Chapter

As Life Will Still
Be Going On For Us!!!

Today, August 8, 2011, after I told Craig and Nicole not to call with any problems, well Craig called the house but I was at the store.

Bob called and said Craig had called and his whole conversation was on the answering machine. He kept asking for me. I guess he was wondering if I had pressed charges on Nicole. Not really sure, maybe because I have talked a lot with him in the past.

The answering machine picked up the whole conversation and it really sounded like he was drunk or high also, didn't make too much sense.

He was stating that Nicole was being suicidal as she has been quite a few times in the past where we had to take her to the hospital and he didn't know what to do.

Bob told him to call 911, that he shouldn't be calling us but to call them. Bob told Craig that he has been through enough suicide attempts that he wasn't buying it.

Bob also told Craig he could call me on my cell phone, but he didn't.

In the meantime I called Nicole and she said she couldn't talk as the Police were there. I told her I wanted to talk to them. She wouldn't let me though.

I was going to tell them she left the Harbors (mental facility) and was not taking her medications, to see if they wouldn't pick her up and take her back as I myself didn't know what was going on as she was avoiding me as she thought I pressed charges on her for taking my necklace.

In the meantime Craig called me and we talked for a while and he goes on and on about her doing all of this. I told him I have had years of this and I had told him once before. He apologized and said he was sorry he didn't believe me as now he thinks I am telling the truth about her being a pathological liar and narcissistic personality. He also told me that she had been raped. But he is no saint either. When he talked to Bob he had mentioned something about hitting Nicole and said he didn't. I asked him, "Did you hit her"?

He was quite for a minute and said he didn't hear me so I repeated myself again. He was a little hesitant but said "No" that he might have grabbed her arm or something.

As I said we talked for a while, I guess letting him vent. Then we hung up.

Later that evening Nicole called and said the cops were called due to him hitting her supposedly (again I can't be sure). But she told me that 2 nights earlier that they had been arguing and they stopped at a convenient store and she got out and ran to the bathroom where he followed her in. She stated that he was choking her and kicked her leg and left a big bruise. The lady running the store called the Police as of all the commotion. Craig left before the Police got there but they took pictures of her then. She stated that he choked her till you could see his fingers on her neck. Police took pictures of that incident and the clerk got the tag number.

Nicole did not press charges that time.

But today when Craig called about the suicidal episode, that was not at all what it was about.

He had taken her phone that he paid for away from her. So outside the place she is staying the people called the cops as they were so loud. It was for hitting her again. So the Police show up and one of them was from the incident that happened 2 nights earlier so he remembered her. So she says. I'm not sure of that either doesn't sound right. This time she said she pressed charges against him. Now I don't know who is telling me the truth but I am just telling you like I heard it, because Craig also lies. Who knows even if the Police were there?

She called the next day and was all excited as she went to apply for a job at the Wing House as she stated she was not going to go back dancing. I told her I saw a new doctor today and he also stated for me to stay away from her as she is my problem. I told her she could talk to me and maybe after going into that program we could work on a better relationship but right now she could call, but no drama.

She stated she called the Social Worker while in Miami and they have her scheduled to go in the program on August 18, 2011. That was the soonest they could get her in. I told her that was the best thing she could do for herself. But we will just have to see if she really does go in, can't believe a word that comes out of her mouth.

So the next night she called and sounded really out of it and I asked her if she was raped. She said she was being hounded by Craig so she went out to do I guess you would call it a trick. She said she got in the car the guy would not give her the money and he forced himself on her while she was fighting to get away. Really a strange phone call to tell me that she went out to have sex for money!!! I thought how much lower she could go, as I thought she would never do anything like that. But being on those pills I think has caused her more brain damage.

The next night she called and it was also a very strange call. She sounded loaded and stated that she slept with a girl. Now I have no idea why she would call me and tell me that. I said what? She said I had a girl spend the night with me and we had sex. I said oh OK. She was slurring a little and then we got cut off. I never called her back as the doctor said to stay away from her.

So now I am waiting for the 18th to come to see if she is going to go to the program that will help her immensely. I pray that she does at least for her own good. I really would hate to loose another child.

Well today is the 17th and I called her to see if she was going in and she said yes. But that is a lie. Because she said she had to call tomorrow which is the 18th and then she will go in Friday. Guess she didn't look at the calendar right or something. After I spoke to her I told Bob I bet she wasn't going to go in and now that I am finishing this and see the date on my computer. NOPE, another big fat lie!!!!

So I really don't know what to expect from her, I really don't. So as I said life will still be going on for us until she does something stupid again or maybe the inevitable. I pray not but it is out of my control as usual.